Heuristic Play

Play in the EYFS

Fully revised and updated to reflect the 2012 EYFS

Contents

Published by Practical Pre-School Books , A Division of MA Education Ltd,
St Jude's Church, Dulwich Road, Herne Hill, London, SE24 0PB. Tel 020 7738 5454
© MA Education Ltd 2009. Revised edition 2013.
www.practicalpreschoolbooks.com

Illustrated by Cathy Hughes. Front cover images: © MA Education Ltd. Photos taken by Sheila Riddall-Leech.

Play in the EYFS: Heuristic Play ISBN: 978-1-909280-28-1

What is heuristic play?

EUREKA!

Think about it

Think about your own learning experiences at school. What learning can you remember that was really effective and why do you think this was? Can you think of any learning experiences that you had that were not successful for you and can you think why this might be? For example, someone can tell you how to drive a car, and you can read up on the subject and look on the internet, but unless you actually get behind the wheel of a car and drive, you will not be successful. Learning to drive requires first-hand experiences.

Play can and does, take many forms. It changes as we grow and develop. In the first instance, play enables us to learn about things and objects in our environment, then later through play, we learn about people, thirdly play makes it possible for us to learn about ourselves. Whether play is alone or in groups, messy, noisy and energetic or quiet, all children benefit from it. Play can be a solitary or social experience, we can be fully involved or just watch and observe, but whatever form it takes it is of immense value and fundamental to learning.

It is widely accepted that play is the primary way that babies and young children develop and learn. Learning is about being able to do something by oneself, such as reaching out and grasping an object, writing your name, understanding the difference between hard and soft, fastening a button. This is often referred to as 'learning through first-hand experiences'. When babies and children learn through play they feel free to experiment, are in control of their own learning and find ways of managing situations, both real and imaginary. Learning through play is fundamental to all areas of a child's development.

Heuristic play is a very simple approach to helping babies and young children learn. The approach uses natural and household objects presented to babies and children so that they can experiment and discover independently. The term 'heuristic play' is often confused with 'holistic play' but the two terms are quite different. Holistic play is when you plan for and meet the needs of the whole child; as in holistic therapies which aim to treat the whole person rather than just the symptoms. For example taking an aspirin may temporarily cure a stress headache, but a holistic treatment would treat the cause, that is to say deal with the stress. The word 'heuristic' originates from the Greek 'eurisko' which means 'I discover' or 'I find'. You may recall the ancient story of Archimedes who leapt out of his bath shouting 'Eureka' as he discovered that his body caused the water level to rise. 'Eureka' simply means 'I have discovered', or 'I understand'.

Heuristic play is an approach for practitioners to follow. It is not a prescription or instruction, in short it is unrestricted and totally child-led. Heuristic play uses natural, recycled household objects that can be found in the home and in the environment. Babies and young children who are engaged in heuristic play explore, find out, investigate and discover for themselves, without active adult intervention. Heuristic play allows babies and young children to make choices and develop preferences and experience play opportunities that are both spontaneous and focused. The National Strategy, 'Early Years – Learning, Playing and Interacting, Good Practice in the Early Years' tells us that playing is a key way in which young children learn as it *'allows children to find out about things, try out and practise ideas and skill, take risks, explore their feelings, learn from mistakes, be in control and think imaginatively.'* (The National Strategy, Early Years – Learning, Playing and Interacting, Good Practice in the Early Years, DfCSF, 2009, p. 9). Heuristic play is one such very effective play opportunity if planned and resourced appropriately.

Heuristic play is open-ended; items and objects can be used and played with in any imaginative way that the child chooses and so there is no 'wrong' or 'right' way to play. Heuristic play can be totally individual as babies and young children react and respond in their own unique and distinctive ways. Children with special needs can engage successfully in heuristic play as it stimulates their senses and is open-ended, rather than prescriptive. What it is not, is an opportunity for the adult to sit back and let the children get on with it. As with any play opportunity it needs careful planning, consideration of health and safety issues and appropriate resources.

Some people also think that heuristic play and treasure baskets are the same thing, when in fact treasure baskets are only one aspect of heuristic play. Treasure baskets, amongst other aspects, will be discussed in more detail in the next chapter.

Think about it

In a way, heuristic play continues throughout our lives as we discover and make sense of new things in our physical world. What do you do when faced with a vegetable or a fruit that you have not seen or even tasted before? You probably touch it with your fingers, turn it over in your hands and feel its texture, you smell it, maybe shake it and listen if it rattles or makes another noise, and you look at it carefully and perhaps taste it. Isn't this heuristic play? It is learning about the fruit from your own first-hand experiences. In fact, any form of scientific enquiry could be described simply as heuristic play.

The role of the adult

The role of the adult in heuristic play is to provide a range of objects – natural, household and recycled – that are safe, hygienic and clean. The adult needs to choose objects that will stimulate interest, exploration and discovery. You will need to set out the objects and make sure that anything used in the play session is safe, not broken or worn out. The adult should be quiet and preferably seated throughout the play session. You need to sensitively observe the children and babies, making a note and listening to their play and be aware of the signs that children have had enough or are losing interest. The end of the session should be unhurried and time should be given for the children to be involved in clearing away the items supported by the adults using simple language and gestures. You will also need to consider:

- When is the best time to set up a heuristic play session
- How long you can allow it to continue
- Where in your setting it can be used
- How often you arrange heuristic play sessions.

All of these points will be covered in greater detail in later chapters.

When offering a treasure basket to a non-mobile baby the adult should be aware that this aspect of heuristic play is a non-social activity in which you will not take part, other than to offer reassurance, smiles and positive body language. Treasure basket play, whilst apparently very simple, offers babies significant and deep experiences, such as making choices, and having control over what they are doing independently. If you become involved and offer a baby a specific object, the play changes as the baby is no longer in control and making their own independent choices.

Case study

Abbie, aged eight months, was presented with a treasure basket for the first time. She immediately set about exploring the objects using all of her senses. The adults in the room at the time had not experienced treasure basket play before and began to offer Abbie different objects and say things such as, 'Abbie look at this brush.' Abbie stopped her independent investigations and took what an adult was offering; but it didn't hold her interest and she soon rejected it for something else. The adults were asked to leave Abbie to explore on her own and they soon began to realise that it was not necessary for them to offer objects and that Abbie was engaged in meaningful play.

Play, whether it is heuristic or another form, can be difficult to define and many researchers and theorists have debated this over the years. What is agreed is that play can be both serious and purposeful or trivial and seemingly purposeless. However, play that is described as 'purposeless' is not really, as babies and children are constantly learning, although it may not be obvious to us. Play is usually personally motivated and children involved are more concerned with what they are doing at that moment rather than future goals or outcomes. It is open-ended and should be free from rules that have been imposed by others, usually adults. The Early Years Foundation Stage (2012) places play very much at the forefront of learning and development.

Elinor Goldschmied (1911-2009) was accredited with first using the term 'heuristic play' in the early 1980s as she observed the exploratory play of babies and toddlers. With other co-workers she discovered that this type of play is experimental as the baby or young child tries to discover what they can do with the object they have found. Goldschmied also advised that heuristic play is not a social activity, as it is concerned with how the individual baby or young child experiments in their own unique way. Obviously, the children will naturally pay attention to each other, maybe copy the actions of another, but their primary focus is on their own discovery and experimentation. Over time, thanks to the continued work of Elinor Goldschmied, heuristic play has become widely recognised as an essential part of understanding the way very young children use a variety of objects to develop abstract thinking, just before the commencement of expressive language.

Elinor Goldschmied was fascinated by detail and undertook countless observations in order to understand and develop practical ways to meet the emergent needs of the youngest children. Current research into the functioning of the brain confirms what Elinor Goldschmied observed. The deep concentration of babies as they use all their senses to explore items in the treasure basket, or heuristic play session, is visible 'outward behaviour', whilst on the inside, the brain is teeming and alive with intense 'neural activity'. Play can be described as nourishing food for the

brain, when presented to babies and young children in an emotionally secure and facilitating environment.

In addition to the work of Elinor Goldschmied other theorists and researchers have advocated the importance of sensory experiences in young children's development.

Jean Piaget's (1896-1980) theory of cognitive development is widely known, and his work about how children learn has been developed and expanded upon. The first stage of his theory, known as the Sensorimotor Stage from birth to about two years, reinforces the belief that children learn through interaction with their immediate environment. For example, a baby sucking a nipple or crawling along the floor is getting varied feedback about their body and its relationship to the environment. In other words, the baby is exploring and investigating the world around them. Heuristic play supports Piaget's theory as the baby explores objects in their own individual way, often retaining the same object for some time or coming back to an object repeatedly as they master and memorise the information that they have discovered. Piaget's theory implies that children should have control over their own learning where they can discover and explore at their own pace. Learning activities therefore have to be open-ended, and in addition should allow the children to play and explore uninterrupted for long periods of time. Again, heuristic play can fulfil these requirements.

Friedrich Froebel (1782-1852) believed that play was a highly significant activity and initiated an approach to learning in early childhood that offers children a wide range of experiences, so that they could develop an understanding of their world and themselves. Again, heuristic play supports

Maria Montessori (1870-1952) believed that children learn best through their own spontaneous activity and that they have a natural inquisitiveness and eagerness to learn. She believed that the role of the adult is to provide an environment which will allow the chid the opportunity to develop skills and concepts, and although much of a Montessori setting will have didactic materials many of them derive from natural materials. Montessori's philosophy was based on scientific observations and she advocated that education begins from birth, with periods of sensitivity when a child is more eager to learn. Heuristic play requires the adult to be a sensitive and attentive observer of the child; Montessori believed that all adult actions should be in response to children's observed behaviours. Furthermore, Montessori thought that children learn best through sensory experiences. For example, she developed ways of teaching letters and numbers using shapes cut out of sandpaper that children could handle and feel.

Margaret McMillan's (1860-1931) views incorporated the theories of both Froebel and Montessori. She gave much importance to children experiencing things for themselves and first hand. She recognised that children could learn much from the natural environment and that children should engage in free play in open spaces, with a wide range of materials and resources.

In more recent times **Tina Bruce**, a leading expert in early childhood education, places great emphasis on the benefits of play. Bruce identifies free-flow play, which is described as a network of related processes which include exploration, manipulation, discovery, effort and practice. All these processes are evident in heuristic play.

The **Reggio Emillia** approach in Northern Italy promotes the idea that children are active participators in their own learning. Multi-sensory activities dominate and children are actively encouraged to be imaginative and expressive. The environment in which the children play is of fundamental importance.

this view. Play and the natural world were of importance to Froebel and young children were encouraged to explore the outdoors and discover things for themselves through the interactions with their environment.

Rudolf Steiner (1861-1925) believed that children learn from what happens all around them, including the environment and the people with whom they interact. In a Steiner setting (Waldorf School) all items will be made from natural materials wherever possible and resources can be used in open-ended and imaginative ways. In a Steiner school the pace of learning is set by the child and play is highly regarded as it supports all aspects of a child's development.

In 'Learning, Playing and Interacting' it states that, *'Babies and young children are powerful learners, reaching out into the world and making sense of their experiences with other people, objects and events. As they explore and learn, children are naturally drawn to play.'* (2009, pg. 3) This reinforces the belief that heuristic play enables children and babies to explore and learn. Children should be offered a wide range of sensory experiences so that they can respond and use movements and explorations to connect with their immediate environment.

A Unique Child is a dominant theme of the EYFS where the baby or young child is in an enabling environment that allows them to develop and learn in different ways

and at different rates. As a child-led play activity, a treasure basket allows a baby to play and learn in their own unique way and at their own pace. A carefully planned and resourced heuristic play session for toddlers shows that the adults involved understand how to create an enabling environment. Links to the EYFS will be discussed in greater detail within the section on each particular age-group.

Linking heuristic play to schemas and learning tools

How children learn and develop has occupied the work of theorists and researchers for centuries. As mentioned earlier, Jean Piaget has been very influential and used very specific terms to describe the learning process. One of these terms is 'schema', a plan or mental structure that allows children to sort out their experiences, without words. Schemas can be likened to pieces of a jigsaw puzzle which children are mentally building and completing. Schemas do not follow predictable patterns and do not appear in any particular order. Some children may have several different schemas at any one time, whilst others may show no evidence of any. Sometimes schemas may only be evident in certain places, such as at home or only in the setting.

More recently, researchers such as Tina Bruce and Chris Athey have continued to look at the way children learn and develop and build upon the work of Piaget, particularly in relation to schemas. Their research shows us that schemas develop in coordinated clusters, based on the senses and movement, to become sophisticated concepts (such as speed). All schemas have two aspects or forms, the configurative form and the dynamic; for example the configurative form of an enclosure is a square, a circle or another shape. The dynamic form is a rotating or moving hoop, or steering wheel. Both are very important for learning. Schemas can be on different levels: sensorimotor, which is dominated by the senses and movement; symbolic representation, which shows in pretend and imaginative play; and functional dependency which is exploring cause and effect.

Although babies begin with the same schema, these develop and match up with each other, as they are influenced by people, objects and cultural influences. Schemas are constantly being adapted and enlarged as we learn more. Babies need the help of adults and other children to assist them to use schemas to learn. We need to be aware of developing schemas and plan activities and experiences based on our observations of what babies and children already know and can do rather than what we think they should be doing.

The chart on page 9 describes some common schemas that you might observe in children and babies' play, but this list is far from exhaustive.

In the DVD *Heuristic Play with Objects* (1992) there are many examples of early schemas in action. All the children in the DVD are between 12 and 20 months and are all mobile. Children can be observed carrying objects around such as large tins from one side of the room to another and at clearing up time carrying objects to the adult to be placed in drawstring bags (transporting). Another child is focused at placing wooden pegs around the sides of a large tin (connecting and positioning), and another places lengths of beads and chains around their neck. One child spends time in pushing corks down the neck of a plastic bottle; an example of early enveloping schema. The adults have provided many objects that roll, such as tubes, hair rollers, tins and plastic bottles so that the children can develop the schema of trajectory and rotation. All the materials that are provided for the children in their heuristic play session can be used in infinite open-ended ways and provide opportunities for filling and emptying, connecting, moving and transporting.

Case study

Toddlers aged between 19 and 26 months were role-playing in a shop area. They transported their 'shopping' in trolleys, bags and baskets as they moved around the 'shop'. One had a doll in a buggy with a bag hooked over the handle, others pretended to take things from the shop and put them into their bags and trolleys, offering 'money' for their purchases.

This clearly shows the schemas of transporting and containing. The three levels of schemas are also evident, the children uses their senses and movement as they transported their 'shopping', they could engage in symbolic representation as they understood pretend play with cards and money, and finally they explored cause and effect (functional dependency) as they moved around the shop adding to their purchases and so making the bags heavier or the buggy more difficult to control.

SCHEMA	DESCRIPTION OF POSSIBLE BEHAVIOURS
Transporting	• Carry all the bricks from one place to another in a bag • The sand from the tray to the role play area in a bucket • Push a friend around in a toy pram or buggy.
Enveloping	• Cover themselves with their flannel when washing • Wrap a doll up in blanket • Wrap objects from a treasure basket in material • Sit in the sand tray and cover their legs with sand • Cover their whole painting with one colour.
Enclosure/containing	• Put their thumb in and out of their mouth • Fill up and empty containers of all kinds, such as trolleys bags, purses, buckets, tins • Climb into large cartons • Sit in the tunnel, build 'cages' with blocks.
Trajectory; Diagonal/vertical/horizontal	• Gaze at your face • Drop things from their baby seat • Make arcs with their spilt food using their hands or with 'messy play' materials such as shaving foam, corn flour and water • Play with the running water in the bathroom • Climb up and jump off furniture • Line up the cars • Make or draw lines • Bounce, throw and kick balls.
Rotation	• Be fascinated by the spinning washing machine • Love anything with wheels, or that will roll, such as balls, tubes • Roll down a hill • Enjoy spinning round or being swung around.
Connection	• Distribute and collect objects to and from a practitioner • Spend time joining the train tracks together • Stick masking tape across from the table to the chair • Join tubes together with lengths of chain.
Positioning	• Put things on their head • Prefer their custard next to their pudding, not over it • Lie on the floor or under the table, and walk around the edge of the sandpit • Select a specific object from a treasure basket and place it carefully on their legs, or at the side.
Transforming	• Add juice to their mashed potato, or sand to the water tray • Enjoy adding colour to corn flour or making dough.
Scattering	• Leave toys around the room • Scatter sand from a height.

In the DVD *Infants at Work* (1989) babies can be seen deliberately placing items so that they can return to them later. They bang two items together to make connections and turn them over and rotate.

Treasure baskets and heuristic play are excellent ways to promote and extend schemas. A sensitive and positive adult can support the constant repetition which can be a feature of any schemas, such as a baby turning a marble egg over and over in their hands. Treasure baskets allow objects to be accessible to babies so that they can freely select and choose as they develop and play.

Learning tools are the earliest patterns of behaviour that emerge in very young babies. All of the learning tools can be clearly observed in the DVD *Infants at Work*, as well as the DVD of the toddlers. They include:

- **Placing** – a baby deliberately places an object to the side so that they can return to it later in the play session.

- **Banging** – in the first instance a baby accidentally bangs two objects together, but repeats this (this is also clearly seen in the DVD *Heuristic play with objects* as two toddlers bang tins and large cans together).

- **Pairing and matching** – a baby holds two similar objects and studies them intently, toddlers seek out objects that are the same to put on a piece of tubing.

- **Sorting** – very clear in the DVD of the toddlers as they pack away the objects and also as the babies 'sort' through the basket for similar objects.

- **Piling** – babies and children put objects deliberately on top of each other, such as tins and cans, blocks and plastic bottles.

- **Sequencing** – the children sequence their activity during play and whilst clearing away.

Both schemas and learning tools overlap and at times blend and combine, sometimes you can observe them in parallel. Heuristic play provides endless opportunities for cognitive development; we learn nothing about our world and environment until we can deliberately pick something up, explore and investigate it. In other words, engage in heuristic play.

What is a treasure basket?

In simple terms, a treasure basket is a collection of natural and household objects which are put into a basket. The basket is put on the floor and babies are allowed to explore its contents. Babies who can sit up, but not yet crawl, can experience heuristic play through a treasure basket. A treasure basket is a simple but very effective way of offering deep and meaningful stimulation to babies.

The treasure basket idea was conceived by Elinor Goldschmied in the early 1970s and has gained in popularity ever since. It offers choice and promotes concentration skills. Babies can choose which items to pick up or not and when to pick them up. Learning how to choose is a very fundamental life skill.

The actual basket should be sturdy and made of wicker or other natural material with no sharp bits or edges. It needs to have rigid sides and be flat bottomed. Ideally, you should aim to have a round basket (but my basket is rectangular in shape and has successfully been used by countless babies). The baskets should be about 12 centimetres in height and 30 centimetres in diameter. However, a baby with shorter arms might be better with a smaller basket. Some practitioners have successfully used a large tin or bowl instead of a basket.

Case study

Poppy, nine-months-old, and Phoebe, seven months, were sat either side of a treasure basket. This was their first experience of a treasure basket and both showed their excitement by vocal sounds and gross motor movements such as waving their arms and moving their legs. Their excitement was also evident in their feet: their toes moved up and down and wiggled. Both of their mums sat behind their babies and every now and then both Poppy and Phoebe looked up and smiled at them. Both mums made reassuring comments and smiled back.

The basket should be placed on the floor at the side of the baby, not in front of them. In this position a baby can more easily access the items and more than one baby can be involved. The adult should be seated to one side of the baby, so that you can see and observe the play, but not in the line of vision of the baby. This is so the baby will interact with the objects and not another person. Holding a baby on your knee with the treasure basket in front of them is not good practice and will not allow the baby to experience the full potential of treasure basket play.

What objects can go into my treasure basket?

You need to start to collect as many objects as possible of different colours, texture, taste, smell, weight and temperature. Plastic objects should be avoided and not included in your treasure basket. The idea is to offer maximum stimulation to the baby's senses, so look for objects to stimulate:

- **Sight** – different colours, form, length and shininess

- **Smell** – a variety of scents

- **Sound** – ringing, tinkling and banging noises

- **Taste** – could be restrictive, but possible

- **Touch** – texture, weight, shape and temperature.

Objects can be made of metal, wood, shell, stone, bristle, raffia, rubber, leather or material, but all should be natural and not derived from plastic. It is good practice to have more than one of each object, such as two wooden spoons, and you should try to have a full basket. In the DVD *Infants at Work* (Goldschmied, E.,1989, NCB) Elinor Goldschmied says that she has over 100 objects in the basket!

List of suggested objects for a treasure basket

Wooden objects

Spoons of all sizes	Cotton reels
Spatulas	Pieces of doweling
Pegs	Honey spoon
Curtain rings	Napkin ring
Egg cup	Door wedge
Cube	Citrus juicer
Wooden ball	Place mat
Corks	Strings of wooden beads
Small rolling pin	Blocks

Metal objects

Bunch of keys	Spoons of all sizes
Scoop	Whisk
Small tins (smooth edges)	Lengths of chains
Bottle brush	Metal egg cup
Tea strainer	Sieve
Plug and chain	Ornament
Set of measuring spoons	Closed tins with pebbles or rice inside
Jar lids	Metal beaker
Bells	

Natural objects

Large pebbles	Shells
Pine cones	Feathers
Lemon	Orange
Apple	Natural sponge
Pumice stone	Large corks
Raffia mat	Bamboo chopsticks

Textiles

Ribbons	Leather purse
Material purse	Woollen pom-poms
Marble eggs	Tennis ball
Bean bag	Lavender bag
Rubber ball	Door stop
Piece of sheepskin	Piece of fur
Cotton facecloth	Silk scarf
Small basket	Short piece of rope

Brushes
(should have wooden/metal handles and natural bristles)

Pastry brush	Bottle brush
Hair brush	Shaving brush
Nail brush	Shoe brushes
Make-up brush	Paint brushes
Vegetable brush	

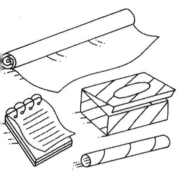

Paper and cardboard

Tubes	Small boxes and cartons
Grease proof paper	Tin foil
Small notebook with spiral rings	Sandpaper

Glass and marble

Decanter stopper	Glass/marble eggs
Make-up mirror	Ornaments
Paper weight	

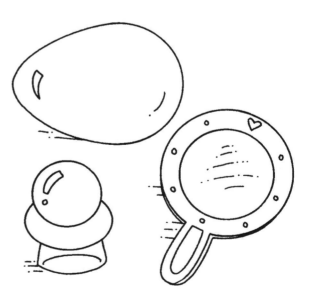

Remember the more variety in the treasure basket, the more motivating and richer the play experience will be for the baby.

PHOTOCOPIABLE PAGES

Practical Pre-School Books
www.practicalpreschoolbooks.com

Caring for objects

The objects that you choose should be hygienic and safe. But what do we actually mean by safe? Everybody has their own views of what constitutes 'safe' based on their own personal experiences. For example, you might consider a bunch of keys quite safe for a baby to explore; but somebody else may have had a baby who had hurt their lips or mouth on the keys and so would consider this object as unsuitable for use in a treasure basket. In the same way you may offer a baby a fir cone that you have found in a woodland area and think it is ideal for your treasure basket; somebody else may think it is unhygienic and dirty and so not offer it.

In terms of cleanliness and objects being hygienic, you should be able to wash the objects as you would do to any other toy that you give to a baby. Use a bowl of hot water with washing up liquid.

Washing objects by hand and rinsing in clean water is an effective way of keeping things clean and hygienic. You can also wipe each object with a sterile wipe, or use a disinfectant spray. Think carefully before using some commercial cleaning products, such as antibacterial sprays – given current research on their effect on very young children in relation to allergies and other medical conditions.

Some natural objects such as feathers and fir cones, paper and card and things made from leather, fur and other textiles will not wash. Such objects can be sterilised very effectively in a microwave, provided there are no metal attachments. Fir cones and feathers for example can be put in a microwave for about 20 seconds without damage to either the object or the oven.

Natural objects can deteriorate more quickly than metal or wood and therefore its important that they are replaced as soon as they start to look worn. Materials can be either washed by hand or in a washing machine.

If you are concerned about the safety of an object then don't include it. Elinor Goldschmied used the words,

Case study

As part of the normal cleaning routine in a day nursery, staff in the baby room tipped out the contents of their treasure baskets after each baby had explored the contents. All wipeable objects were cleaned over with 'baby wipes'. Anything that had deteriorated, was damaged or had loose bits, was taken out and thrown away and the remaining objects were taken to the kitchen area and either washed in warm soapy water, rinsed and left to dry, or popped into the microwave for a few seconds. Although this aspect of their routine took a bit more time, it prevented cross-infection and so helped keep the babies safe.

'washable, wipeable or disposable': a very sound rule to follow.

You need to think about where you are going to keep your treasure basket when not in use. The basket itself is a natural container and you don't need to put it into anything else. The basket should be easily accessible as other resources would be. You don't want the objects to get dusty or mixed up with other equipment so it is a good idea to cover the basket when not in use.

Beginning your collection

When you start to make your treasure basket collection you must check every object very carefully.

- Look for sharp edges, loose bits and splits or cracks, especially on natural objects such as pine cones, pebbles or shells.
- Check bristles on a brush to make sure that they are not loose and likely to come out.
- Make sure that the lids on tins are tight and the contents of the tin cannot spill out.

- Look carefully at the basket itself, feel the edges, and make sure that there are no sharp bits. Make sure the basket is rigid and firm.
- Objects that you take from around your home must be clean and in top quality condition. For example, a metal whisk is an ideal object for a treasure basket provided that it is not possible to slide the handle down and so expose the sharp metal ends. If you buy a new metal whisk it is unlikely that you would be able to move the handle, but one that you have had in your kitchen for a while may have worked itself loose.
- Feel all wooden objects carefully to make sure that they are smooth and do not have splinters. Some very cheap wooden spoons are not smooth and you may need to rub them over with an emery board or sandpaper. This also applies to the handles of some brushes.

Some common worries

Some practitioners and parents have genuine concerns about allowing a baby to play with some of the objects in a treasure basket. They believe that objects could be dangerous, dirty, unsuitable and inappropriate or the babies could harm themselves. However, babies of this age can hold and grasp objects but are unlikely to be able to poke, jab or hit another baby.

These are real and valid fears and should not be dismissed lightly, but can be discussed and shared. Some common worries are:

Objects might be sharp
There are many objects in the treasure basket that could be sharp and so could possibly scratch a baby, for example a tin or the edges of a shell. It is often the case that people will not put objects into a treasure basket because they themselves have been hurt by them, but babies are extremely cautious when exploring objects, particularly if the object is new. But, if you are really careful about maintaining and replacing objects, such as shells, which can become brittle and therefore a hazard, there should be no problem.

Case study

The baby room leader of a day nursery attended training on using treasure baskets and decided to introduce the idea to the rest of the staff. She put a list up on the wall of objects to collect and asked all staff and parents to help collect as many as possible. Each time an object was brought in, the leader marked it on the list. Everyone became involved; for example 'dolly pegs' used by a baby's grandmother were brought in, one parent went through his key cupboard and put all the keys that he wasn't using on to single keyrings, one staff member's family kept chickens and so provided a regular supply of feathers. Within two weeks the leader had almost 100 different objects and so treasure basket play could begin. Because parents had been involved, many were very interested in how their babies would play with the objects and so lots of photographs were taken (with written permission) so the parents could see the benefits. Several parents also started their own collections for play at home.

Case study

Poppy discovered a metal whisk in the treasure basket. Her mum admitted that normally Poppy would not be allowed to play with it because of a fear that she could hurt her mouth. However, Poppy explored the whisk for over 15 minutes, feeling the handle with her tongue, putting her fingers through the whisk, banging it on the basket, on the floor and against lots of other objects. Her delight in her explorations was evident as she vocalised her pleasure and moved her whole body, including her toes.

Objects might break

All toys might break at some point and you would automatically throw them away. The same is true for all objects in a treasure basket and so you should check the contents of your basket frequently. It is also important to remember that babies exploring objects rarely have the strength and physical skills to throw a glass paper weight with enough force to break it. And why would they want to throw it when their main interest is to explore and discover the attributes of that glass object?

Babies swallowing or choking on objects

When people see babies putting objects into their mouths they often think that the baby will choke, however many objects in the basket would be impossible for an adult to swallow, never mind a baby. You should remember that when a baby explores and mouths objects they rarely put the object right inside their mouth. We sometimes get the impression that an object is right inside the mouth and so become fearful of choking, but often our fears are unnecessary. Look carefully at the objects in your treasure basket and ask yourself could you swallow or choke on them. If the answer is yes then obviously the object is too small for a baby. Do not make the mistake of putting objects that are too big in your treasure basket because you are fearful the baby could swallow small things. For

example don't put in the cardboard tube from a roll of tin foil etc. which is about 30 cm long; it would be better to cut the tube into four lengths of between 7 and 8 cm.

Hazards and risks of handles

Many objects in the treasure basket such as a whisk, spoon, bottle brush and some sieves have thin handles, which a few people think a baby would push too far down their throat or use to poke themselves in the eye, ear or nose. A non-mobile baby's grip is not particularly sophisticated and it is unlikely that they could coordinate their actions sufficiently to connect with their eye, ear or nose. The main focus of treasure basket play is exploration of the objects, using sensory information; the baby concentrates intently on the object in their hand and large physical movements which would be needed to push objects down their throat or poke into their eye, ear or nose rarely, if ever, occur. Admittedly, accidents can happen, but the adult should be carefully observing the play and would intervene at any point that they felt the baby was at risk.

You must remember that your anxieties and fears about objects can be picked up by the baby and this could have a detrimental effect on the quality of play. The fears are yours, not the baby's and you need to think about the reasons why you have these anxieties; is it past personal experience that has caused your anxiety?

When to have a treasure basket session

As this is a relatively easy session to set up and there is quite a lot of flexibility for the adult responsible. Don't produce the treasure basket as a time-filler at the end of the day, or just before feeding or nap time; you will be giving the activity a limited chance of success. A time when parents are coming in to collect other babies or children is not good either. Babies need plenty of time to settle and concentrate on any activity and should be emotionally calm and content. Your session should be at a time when you can be reasonably sure that there will be around half an hour of peaceful and uninterrupted play. If you can, it is good practice to offer a treasure basket on a daily basis, or each time that the baby is in your setting.

Some babies can concentrate for surprisingly long periods when exploring a treasure basket, so make sure that you can organise between 30 minutes and an hour for the activity. However, if a baby is only interested for 10 or 15 minutes, accept that this the baby's limit and find another activity to attract their interest and attention.

The role of the adult

Any heuristic play session needs to be as carefully planned as any other activity in your setting, and so it is important that all adults involved understand their role. Elinor Goldschmied was quite specific about the role of adults and how the role could be misinterpreted due to an apparent lack of involvement. We are often told that we should become actively involved in children's play experiences in order to develop and extend their ideas and learning, however active involvement is not required during a treasure basket play session. That does not mean that you can sit back and do nothing. In the words of the EYFS you should 'look, listen and note' during the session.

The role of the adult should be:

- To collect and accumulate a wide variety of safe and hygienic objects to go in to the treasure basket.

Think about getting the support of colleagues and parents to help you gather as large a range of objects as possible.

- To check each object for safety and cleanliness and take appropriate action.
- To plan a suitable time for the treasure basket activity, making sure that there is sufficient time for the baby to concentrate uninterrupted. You will also need to think about if your timing suits the baby's needs and routines. Check that the baby is comfortable, not hungry, tired or needing a nappy change.
- To make sure that the floor space to be used is clean and safe.
- To make sure that the floor space is in an area that is quiet and if possible free from distractions, such as older children, and preferably carpeted.
- To position themselves on a chair if possible, from which they can closely observe the baby and offer quiet reassurance and support.
- To be comfortable and relaxed so that they can be attentive, quiet, interested and responsive with the baby.

- To respond with smiles and gestures to the baby's pleasure and interest in the objects in the basket.

The adult should not:

- Attempt to direct the play by offering objects to the baby
- Talk to the baby and distract them or disturb their concentration.
- Talk to other adults whilst the babies are engrossed in the treasure basket play, as this will not allow you to observe and respond to the baby.
- Regard the session as a time to catch up on paper work or another activity. Doing this means that you are not focusing on the baby and their learning.

Links to the Early Years Foundation Stage

One of the most significant features of a treasure basket is that it allows a baby to learn how to make independent choices as they explore the objects. For example, the choice of which object to choose and how to explore and play with it gives a baby the opportunity for independent thinking which is the starting point of expressive arts and design. ('Development Matters' in the Early Years Foundation Stage 2012, p. 43.)

Babies have strong investigative and examining urges and the treasure basket provides endless opportunities to satisfy these. This links directly to the EYFS area of learning and development of **Personal, Social and Emotional Development**. Babies are able to develop self-confidence and self-esteem as they actively explore the objects. They can freely express their pleasure, delight, excitement and even frustration as they explore; remove a baby's socks as they sit by the treasure basket and watch how they express their feelings through the whole of their body and their little toes wiggle in sheer delight or excitement! We often think that young babies play in a solitary way, which is in most cases true, however babies will engage in short social interactions during treasure basket play.

Case study

Poppy and Phoebe were engaged in exploring a treasure basket. Poppy was quite vocal and she explored and discovered different objects; Phoebe on the other hand was relatively quiet. However, Phoebe would sit and watch Poppy intensely and then copy her actions. Both babies reached towards each other and tried to grasp an object, once or twice Poppy took an object from Phoebe, but she just confidently reached for another object from the basket.

Babies will communicate in a variety of ways as they explore the contents of the treasure basket. Not only will they wiggle their toes, but will also make sounds with their voices, gurgling, squealing and babbling to express their feelings and communicate with a sensitive and caring adult. In 'Development Matters', page 15, it is suggested that practitioners create an environment for the youngest children which invites responses from babies such as touching, smelling, feeling, exploring. Even before they can talk in words, babies express their ideas through sounds, gestures and body language. Heuristic play will provide excellent opportunities for non-verbal communication. Babies will explore the objects in a treasure basket that catch their attention for sustained periods when undisturbed and in an enabling environment. This is **active learning** (Statutory Framework for Early Years Foundation Stage, page 7: 'active learning-children concentrate and keep on trying') as babies test things, solve problems and gain a sense of satisfaction from their play.

Babies' mathematical development begins as soon as they begin to make connections and notice differences and similarities between the objects in the basket. They can develop an awareness of shape, texture and form as they play. When there is more than one type of object in the treasure basket, such as two metal spoons or two wooden balls, babies will begin to be aware that there is more than one; the beginnings of using numbers as labels and for counting. This links to the area of learning and development – **Mathematics**.

Exploration and Investigation are aspects of **Understanding the World**, and therefore a treasure basket is an excellent activity for this area of learning and development. The earliest stages of design and making are as a baby explores objects with their hands and mouths. The different textures and materials within the basket provide endless opportunities for a baby to explore and investigate in a safe way, to sort and test out the properties of the materials offered. The more you fill your basket and the greater variety of objects you put in the better the learning experience. Don't forget you can duplicate objects as well.

As babies pick up, handle and grasp a range of objects their physical skills and dexterity will be stimulated and developed. This of course links to **Physical Development**. Treasure basket play will also stimulate hand/eye coordination, control, fine motor and manipulative skills. Sitting alongside the basket will help the baby gain upper body strength, balance and control

Expressive Arts and Design, as mentioned earlier, are about making choices; it is also about responding to the environment in a variety of ways, and in particular through the senses. Creative development is not about producing an end product, such as finger painting to 'take home'; it is a process that is open-ended. Children will be more able to make connections between things later on in their learning and education if they have had opportunities to explore independently, and that is exactly what treasure basket play is all about.

Observation and assessment suggestions and links to schemas

Observation is the recognized word for one of the most important aspects of our everyday work. Observing babies

and children is something we do constantly and is how we make professional judgments and assessments about their needs, learning and development. Many of us observe almost instinctively and find it difficult to record these intuitive thoughts and judgements. It can help to have an aim or focus area to think about whilst observing, and so plan appropriate activities for the future.

All planning should start with observing children so that we can organise and arrange appropriate and purposeful activities. The EYFS places a great importance on looking, listening and noting so that we can put the child at the centre of our practice. However, it is important to remember that one observation is never sufficient to provide enough evidence for making meaningful assessments and judgments. Treasure basket play, in which we are not actively involved, provides boundless opportunities for us to observe, take photographs, (with written parental permission) and assess development.

Observations should be focused, and planned in advance, for example: 'today I am going to observe Jess aged 8 months during a treasure basket session and make a note of how she makes choices'. This actually helps other staff to organise their time and know that you will be involved in observations and so, if possible, should not be interrupted. Observations can be quite spontaneous, such as during a treasure basket play session you may notice a baby making deliberate attempts to place and position objects and so decide to record the evidence of this developing schema.

How we record our observations very much depends on the situation and the context of the activity. At the back of this book are two photocopiable **observation and planning proforma sheets**, which could be used during treasure basket play sessions. On the first sheet you could

record a summary of several observations in the box at the top left and link this across to the areas of learning and development. From this box an arrow leads you to the bottom right where you can reflect on and think about the skills observed. An arrow leads you to the next box on the bottom left where you can record possible activities for the next steps and so this leads you back to observing, thus completing the planning cycle.

The second planing sheet begins with the child at the heart of everything we do: what are their interests, likes and dislikes. These are briefly recorded in the centre circle. In the middle circle you could plan activities based on the information in the centre. In the outer circle you can observe each activity and link it to the EYFS. In the middle circle it is a good idea to always have one activity which does not vary, such as treasure basket play. This is usually referred to as continuous provision and ensures that you offer a consistent experience for the child to encourage emotional security. It is not intended that this sheet would be completed in one day, but could be used over a longer period of time.

Suggestions for observations:

- Watch how a baby handles each object: which grasp do they use, do they use one or both hands, do they turn

the object over? This would include fine motor and fine manipulative skills.

- Do they explore more than one object, maybe one held to the mouth and another in the hand?
- Observe the baby's levels of concentration, how is this evident? Look at body language, gestures, facial expressions and vocalisations.
- Watch how a baby expresses their feelings. (Remember the wiggly toes!) Make a note of their body language, facial expressions, gestures and vocalisations.
- What feelings and emotions can you observe: pleasure, excitement, frustration?
- Look for evidence of schemas such as:
  - Positioning: a baby may for example place an object carefully by their legs so that they can return to it again.
  - Orientation: turning objects and placing them.
  - Connection: banging two objects together.
  - Rotation: focusing on things that turn, such as knobs or balls.

Case study

Flynn, nine-months-old, has been offered treasure basket play sessions at least three times a week since he was able to sit unaided. His key person, Ali, had observed him many times, focusing on how Flynn made choices, developed attention, physical skills and schemas such as positioning. Using the observation notes, Ali planned activities and experiences that would develop Flynn's learning and skills, for example he played with shaving foam, which helped extend his schema of trajectory as he made large movements with the foam. Flynn was also offered resources which he could safely bang together to relate to the specific learning tools of banging and connecting schema.

What do they need?

As soon as babies begin to make independent attempts to move and crawl, the world becomes a very different place. Crawling is not just a physical activity; the brain and therefore cognitive development, is also stimulated. New possibilities present themselves; the baby can not only move themselves about, but can also move objects from one place to another. They can see the world from a different perspective and can begin to develop spatial awareness. Their explorations and investigations will require more space, and this will have implications for adults' planning and resourcing.

Obviously the point at which a baby begins to move about depends on their own individual rate of development. Not all babies go through a crawling on all fours stage, some shuffle, and some may have a very short period of crawling before they attempt to walk. You will need to use your own professional judgements based on observations as to when you need to offer more than a treasure basket.

A treasure basket can still be offered to a toddler in this age group; perhaps when a child is feeling tired or not particularly well they will often benefit from playing with something familiar. At times such as these, all children need the reassurance of a sensitive and caring adult and so the treasure basket can be a source of comfort, especially if it is used on a one-to-one basis. In these circumstances you could talk to the toddler about the objects and interact more than you would normally do if the basket was being offered to a baby.

Sometimes early years practitioners can find it a challenge to plan appropriate activities and experiences for this age group. Many toddlers have become disinterested in 'baby toys', but are not yet mature enough to be involved in activities planned for older children. The second year of a baby's life is one of extraordinary growth and development; but Elinor Goldschmied believed that sometimes the experiences and activities offered at this time, especially in group care, can be limiting. This is where heuristic play can really be very beneficial.

Heuristic play for this age group requires collections of recycled and household objects, a variety of sizes, shapes, textures and materials. In this way the toddler will still continue to explore and investigate through their sensory experiences but will also be able to extend their learning. This form of play is quite active compared to treasure basket play, but with the same purpose and concentration.

In the first instance you can offer the treasure basket together with some large tins, boxes or similar containers. You will find that the baby will independently discover that they can drop things into the containers. If you watch the baby, they will probably tip them out again and so discover the concept of 'in and out' and 'here and there'; schemas of positioning, enveloping and cause and effect.

As with the treasure basket there is no place for plastic toys. Most plastic toys offer very limited sensory experiences and also will frequently have a single or correct way of playing with them. For example, a plastic shape sorter will only have one place where each shape can be posted. What often happens is that the toddler will transport the shape to a different place and post it somewhere that an adult may consider inappropriate or 'wrong' and then the whole toy could become uninteresting to the child.

With heuristic play there is no right or wrong; there is no sense of failure. The toddler is able to experiment and

Case study

Lucy, aged 15 months, took a little while to begin to explore the heuristic play materials and returned several times to the adult nearby for support. She discovered that she could pile several different objects on top of each other; she used different sized tins, plant pots and plastic bottles. She squealed in delight as the pile of objects fell over, but immediately started rebuilding her pile.

investigate freely as to what they can do with the objects. They will learn and discover different outcomes to their experiments, for example a cork may fit into a plastic bottle, but may not come out very easily, whereas the same cork can be put inside a tin and taken out again with little effort. These different outcomes will stimulate the toddler's thinking and so help them develop a greater understanding of the objects and their characteristics.

In a heuristic play session a toddler needs to be able to do the following:

- Move or transport objects from one place to another in a variety of ways.
- Put objects inside other containers and take them out again, including smaller objects inside bigger ones.
- Roll objects across the floor or over different surfaces
- Bang objects together, sometimes connecting, sometimes not.
- Make piles of objects and then knock them over, sometimes similar objects sometimes just random choices.
- Make collections of similar objects.
- Turn and twist objects either inside each other or in their hands.
- Wrap objects up in materials, including putting things over themselves.

Not only can all of the above be recognised as schemas (as discussed earlier in the book) or learning tools, the basis of problem solving can be identified as well. For example, when a toddler bangs two or more objects together, they will initially use one hand. This later develops into a two-handed action which is often rhythmic and involves large body

Case study

Lucy and Oliver explored the heuristic play materials at the same time. Lucy, the younger toddler, watched Oliver intently and copied some of his actions. She picked up a tube copying Oliver and made noises down the tube as he had done. She watched as he put plant pots on his head and tried to copy him. Although very aware of each other, neither toddler made any attempt to play together.

movements. This will eventually lead to the use of tools, and later to writing and drawing.

As with a treasure basket, heuristic play does not depend on adult intervention and can be a solitary activity. Toddlers will play and explore independently but at the same time will probably be aware of the actions of others. They may play and explore in parallel. They may well copy each other's actions, such as banging two objects together and may laugh at the noise they are making, but will not play together.

Levels of concentration, because of the wealth of experiences and opportunities for exploration are vast, are usually high. This is often regarded as unusual, as toddlers of this age are easily distracted. Children with special or additional needs may also lack the ability to concentrate and can be easily sidetracked or have their attention diverted. Heuristic play for these children can be especially valuable and meaningful as the very act of exploring the range of materials can be absorbing and so promote concentration skills.

During heuristic play sessions the baby and toddler will move through various stages:

- The first stage is: what is this object? What is it like? At this stage the treasure basket can meet this level of enquiry as the baby touches, feels, smells and mouths objects. This stage will also occur in a heuristic play session, especially if new materials are offered.

- During the second stage the baby has a good idea of the characteristics of the objects and materials and so begins to consider what they can do with the objects. This could, for example, involve a toddler putting a tube to their mouth and making noises, putting smaller objects into a big tin and shaking it, putting corks in a bottle etc.
- Finally, as language begins to develop a toddler will engage in what Piaget called 'symbolic play' as they become interested in what an object could become. This could be a length of chain becoming a necklace, or chains in a tin becoming a drink. (Both evident in the DVD *Heuristic Play with Objects*, 1992, NCB).

What do you need to collect?

Before you begin to make your collection you will have to decide how and where you will store the objects. For many settings storage is an issue and 15 large tins can be quite a challenge to store safely. In the DVD *Heuristic Play with Objects* you will see that the adults have several large, fabric drawstring bags in which collections of objects are stored. These bags are then hung on hooks, which keeps them clean and dust free. Large tins and containers are stored on shelves. When I began my collection, I made several fabric bags and stored items in them. I did not have room for another shelf in the storage area and so bought some large stacking plastic boxes with lids. We, or rather the toddlers, put all the containers inside each other to save space

and we put everything, including the drawstring bags, in the boxes which could then be stacked on top of each other and so save space.

This was not really ideal, but a solution to our storage problem. The toddlers could still be involved in clearing away the objects and materials and the drawstring bags kept each collection separate.

You will need to collect about 50 of the same type of object and about 15 different collections, for a group of five or six toddlers to play at the same time; that means 50 wooden pegs, 50 shells, 50 containers of different sizes and material and so on. Elinor Goldschmied suggested that three large tins for each toddler was probably sufficient (DVD *Heuristic Play with Objects*).

Think about it

If you have toddlers in your setting observe them during a non-heuristic play session. Make a note of how long they play with the toys provided, or how many different toys that access in say, 45 minutes. Then set up a heuristic play session and compare the concentration levels of the toddlers.

List of suggested objects for a treasure basket

Containers of various sizes and shapes

Cardboard boxes

Wide-necked plastic bottles

Tins

Baskets

Wooden boxes

Flower pots

Yoghurt pots

Seed trays

Objects that will stack

Wooden bricks

Wooden offcuts that have been sanded down

Sets of mats or coasters

Nests of boxes or tins (see above)

Kitchen roll holders with curtain rings

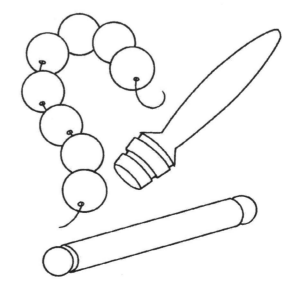

Objects that will roll

Balls of all sizes and different materials

Empty electrical cable spools

Wheels

Tubes

Woollen pom poms

Household and recycled objects

Dolly pegs	Hair rollers
Door knobs	Lengths of chain
Door stops	Jar lids
Curtain rings, wood and metal	Assorted ribbons
Tubing	Cotton reels
Cardboard tubes	Large spoons
Very large buttons	1 metre lengths of silk, lace, velvet

Natural objects

Pine cones	Shells
Pebbles	Seasonal fruits and nuts (check for allergies)

Objects for carrying and transporting

Bags of various sizes and materials	Ice cube trays
Wallets and purses	Colanders
Saucepans	Egg boxes

PHOTOCOPIABLE PAGES

PRACTICAL Pre-School Books
www.practicalpreschoolbooks.com

Case study

Oliver, aged 22 months, discovered a collection of jar lids. He soon discovered that some lids would fit inside each other and some would not. He sat very still for several minutes whilst he discovered which lids would fit and rejected those that would not. Later in the session he discovered different sizes of plant pots and he applied his earlier discoveries to the pots; investigating which ones would fit inside each other and which ones wouldn't.

Try to collect objects and materials that will help to develop concepts and language, for example, objects that are heavy and light, solid and hollow, big and little, long and short. Even though the toddler probably can not verbally express what they are doing, through heuristic play they will begin to develop understanding of these different concepts. Once a toddler has explored and discovered through play that a little object will fit inside a big object, that concept or idea will remain and can be developed. The toddler will understand that big things cannot go inside little things and that some things are the same size. These concepts can then be applied to other situations.

Caring for objects

The way that you care for heuristic play objects is exactly the same as for a treasure basket (as mentioned earlier). Caring for these objects will take longer and so it is important that you have clear policy in your setting about the cleaning and maintenance of the play materials. Natural, household and recycled objects will deteriorate more rapidly than, say, rubber balls. Cardboard tubes can flatten, shells crack and splinter and plastic bottles do not last forever. You can not expect toddlers to have a rich play experience if you offer them inferior or damaged materials. Try to collect and replace such objects as an ongoing activity. That way you will be able to maintain the

Case study

Justine, a childminder, has used heuristic play and treasure baskets effectively for many years. Some babies and toddlers sleep in the late morning and she offers the session after they have eaten lunch. Those who sleep in the afternoon have the sessions after Justine has collected children from school. The school-aged children have different activities and so the heuristic play sessions can be almost free from interruptions at this time of day. Justine starts to encourage the toddlers to clear the objects away about 15 minutes before the end of the session. Justine tries to offer these play sessions each time a minded child is with her, which could be every day or three days a week.

quantity of objects. It is a good idea to have a list on your parents' notice board asking them to bring in heuristic play materials, that way you should have a steady supply to help you restock and replace objects.

When to have a heuristic play session

It is important that this play session can be at a time when there are no distractions or disruptions, such as parents collecting children. Children need to be able to concentrate, so should not be tired or hungry, or need a nappy change. Many practitioners find that just after a nap time can be a good period in the day, or after they are settled first thing in a session. Sessions need to be around an hour long so that the clearing up can be unhurried and calm.

Clearing away is an important part of the heuristic play session and you should plan for about 15 minutes or so for the toddlers and the adult to tidy away the objects. Clearing away time is important and is in fact an extension of the heuristic play sessions and so should be valued. Like the actual play session clearing away should be calm and unhurried so that both children and adults have a sense of completion and satisfaction. When you start to tidy away the objects make sure that you give the message to the children by demonstrating what is expected of them, rather than asking any pointless questions such as, 'Who will help me tidy up?'.

The role of the adult

Setting up a heuristic play session for a group of toddlers will take time and the objects should ideally be arranged without any children around. The toddlers need to be able to move around freely and safely, select their own objects and investigate and explore without the worry of bumping into each other. It is good practice to try to define the play area with furniture or similar, and have a carpet or rug on the floor. This can help to create a calm and quiet environment. Other play materials should not be left in the area to be used for heuristic play, as these could be a distraction.

Try to place collections of objects together, for example all the tins in one area, wooden blocks in another and so on. You can drape lengths of chain over tins or put 'dolly pegs' around a tin. Stand some tubes up; leave others flat on the floor. Make sure that each collection of objects and materials are well spaced out and not too close to something else. You shouldn't just tip everything out of the bags on to the floor and so create a muddle. This will confuse the toddlers – they won't be able to sort materials out and so their explorations and discoveries will be limited.

Given the length of a heuristic play session, you could be sitting still and quietly attentive for a long period of time. It may be stating the obvious, but make sure that you are comfortable; sitting on a chair that is designed for a small child is not good and will give you backache. This means that you will probably wriggle and fidget and in doing so could interrupt the concentration of the toddlers. You should also be able to make a note of what you observe, so not only should you prepare the materials for the children, you also need to prepare materials for yourself, such as the observation template at the back of this book.

Your role is very similar to that described in the previous chapter: you need to be unobtrusive, quietly attentive and observant. There are, however some slight distinctions between treasure basket play and heuristic play sessions:

- A treasure basket is planned for one or two babies, but a heuristic play session could involve several toddlers at any one time. There is more chance therefore that they may bump into each other as they move around, so you need to be observant and gently guide children if they are at risk of a bump.

- Toddlers are unable to share, they simply do not understand the concept of sharing. There is a greater possibility that two children may want the same object; this is where it is vitally important that you provide a large quantity of objects. If two toddlers are attempting to explore for example the same tube or length of chain, the adult can discreetly lean forward and offer another tube or length of chain and so avoid a possible issue. It is not necessary to say anything to the toddlers. In most cases the toddlers will just accept the offered object and will continue to play and explore.

- As the children play and move objects, the materials available will inevitably become mixed-up. Every now and then you can reorganise the objects so that the toddlers can see them better and in doing so you will probably stimulate another idea for investigation.

- As with any play session there may be times when a child accidentally hurts themselves or seeks reassurance from the adult. You should be able to respond quickly but quietly, calmly and gently, to the toddler by remaining attentive throughout the session.

- Sometimes a toddler will become frustrated with what they are trying to do, such as push corks into a plastic bottle. You can carefully intervene and offer either smaller corks or a wider necked bottle. Again, there is no real need to say anything as you offer different objects. The toddler will either accept or refuse them; this does not matter as this is the child's independent choice and all part of their learning and development.

- During the clearing away time you can name the objects that you want the child to bring you for each

bag. When the child responds, you should also give positive praise, such as 'thank you'. As you name each object the child will begin to associate the word with the object and, as they have gained through their play direct sensory experiences of the object, knowing its name acquires real meaning.

- If you also add short, unambiguous comments associated with clearing away such as, 'Bring me another cork', or tube, or 'There is one by the chair', you will also contribute to the development of the child's language, vocabulary and concepts.

Believe in the philosophy of heuristic play and be enthusiastic about its benefits to a child's overall development and learning. Some of your colleagues and parents may be sceptical about its benefits and often have concerns about the objects and materials used. Some people do not appreciate the value of your role as you appear to sit and be uninvolved with the children. You must try to convince these people of the benefits of heuristic play, and there are several ways that you can do this. Most parents and adults recognise the scenario of a young child receiving a present and playing with the box and wrapping paper more than the contents of the present, so to a certain extent you are at a great advantage. Share your observations with colleagues and parents and discuss with them what is evident. Take photographs, with written parental permission, so you can show and talk to the parents about what the children are doing with the objects. Talk about the value of free exploration and discovery and how it lays firm foundations for later learning and development. Finally, encourage parents to begin to make their own collections at home and so experience the play first hand.

Links to the Early Years Foundation Stage

Personal, social and emotional development, like all areas of learning and development, is integrated into the other seven areas, and it can be difficult to separate different

Case study

Lily, aged 16 months, understood many words, but apart from 'Bye bye, no, mummum, dada, me, and dink' she didn't say very much else, but had many gestures in her repertoire to communicate her needs. During a heuristic play session she was observed putting wooden blocks into a large tin and shaking it to make a noise. Her pleasure was evident in the expression on her face. The adult smiled at Lily and acknowledged her pleasure. Lily carried on putting blocks into the tin and started saying 'In, in' each time. Later on in the session Lily tried to get into a large box; this time accompanied by the words 'Me in'. This was the first time that she had used two words together and it was the belief of the adult that the heuristic play session that provided the opportunity for this key aspect of Lily's language development.

The clearing-up session towards the end of the play session provided excellent opportunities for Lily to show that she could understand simple requests (Language for Thinking). When asked to get hair rollers and put them in the bag, Lily did exactly that, followed by wooden blocks. She was asked to get a big tin and bring to the other side of the room and she could understand what was required.

Me in!

aspects. However, the following points are all aspects of this important area of learning and development. A toddler has a natural instinct to explore and find out what they can do. By now, they have an understanding that they are unique and separate beings and can play in distinctly different ways with the same materials. They are able to express in a variety of ways their likes and dislikes.

As you observe heuristic play sessions you will begin to be aware of some toddlers making deliberate choices of materials to explore and so develop favourite things. They get excited about their own achievements and so it is important that you can acknowledge and praise their successes. This will help build self-confidence and self-esteem. As they help with clearing the objects and materials away they will begin to develop an awareness of routines and self-care.

Children develop language at a rapid rate during their second year. They have a strong impulse to communicate frequently, trying out new sounds and words. It states in 'Development Matters' (page 6) that one of the characteristics of effective learning is when children use their senses to explore the world around them. A clear endorsement for heuristic play! Toddlers use language to communicate their likes and dislikes, which objects they want and will use words and sounds to supplement their explorations.

Mathematics is underpinned by the ability to make connections, look for and create patterns, sort and match using a variety of criteria. Heuristic play provides endless opportunities for toddlers to discover connections, make different collections of objects and sort and match. In the above case study Lily, was making connections between the blocks going into the tin and the noise she could create. As they help with clearing the materials and objects away, toddlers are sorting and matching. Again in the case study Lily could differentiate between the hair rollers and the cotton reels, between the wooden blocks and the wooden off-cuts. She was sorting and matching as she cleared away.

practice and develop new skills. All of this learning can be classified as part of physical development and is by trial and error, firsthand experiences. The tidying and clearing away at the end of the heuristic play session not only helps with self-confidence and self-help skills, but also helps toddlers to sequence their actions and learn different ways of handling materials.

Heuristic play is a creative experience; there are no end products, nothing to take home to show parents. Creative development focuses on children finding things out for themselves through sensory experiences and responding in different and unique ways. Exploring materials is an aspect of creative development, and heuristic play strongly reinforces this aspect of development and allows for imagination to be stimulated. (Think about Oliver with the jar lids and plant pots on page 26.)

Observation and assessment suggestions and links to schemas

Observing children allows us to see the child as an individual, not as part of a group (such as babies, or toddlers), especially in large day care or group settings. Recognising and acknowledging each unique child means that we can put the child at the centre of our practice and find out about their specific needs. Observing children helps us to identify their likes and dislikes and their responses to different situations; with this knowledge we can plan more meaningful, experiences and activities that will stimulate their growth and development. Remember, one observation will never give you enough information to base professional judgements and assessments, regardless of what format your observation takes.

Many adults involved in heuristic play sessions have observed young children totally absorbed in their own explorations for long periods of time, such as 30–40 minutes, often without any adult being directly involved. Adults can observe deep and meaningful play taking

Heuristic play enables toddlers to concentrate and focus for long periods of time. An aspect of knowledge and Understanding the World is exploration and investigation and this requires children to be able to concentrate and focus on one thing for a period of time. A well-planned heuristic play session allows a toddler to play at their own pace and so concentrate and focus as they investigate and problem solve. Some of the materials will allow toddlers to design and create their own structures, for example piling tins on top of each other, mixing tins and boxes and tubes to create structures, as Lucy did in the earlier case study. Some toddlers will push and pull the bigger containers and so discover the concepts of movement and spatial awareness.

Heuristic play can offer physical challenges for children as they play with materials of different sizes. This will help them to develop balance, gross motor skills, control of their bodies and coordination. The session will also provide time for the toddler to repeat actions, as well as place in a calm and peaceful environment. It can also be noted how few squabbles and conflicts occur between the toddlers, mainly due to the profusion of materials to explore, but there are many friendly and sociable exchanges and communication between them. All of these observations provide valuable evidence for future planning.

Suggestions for observations:

- Observe toddlers when presented with new materials, do they engage in the first stage of play, as described earlier in the section on play, to determine what the object is, as they did with treasure basket objects?
- Look for evidence of the second stage of play and how children adapt their original ideas of what they can do with an object to 'What else can I do?'.
- Try to do an event sample to record the friendly exchanges between a small group of children. Record how they communicate with each other, and what they are doing.
- Observe toddlers during clearing away and make a note of how the children respond to the directions and instructions given by another adult.
- Observe how the toddlers sort out minor conflicts of interest: do they find another similar object or do they need adult help?
- Look for symbolic play and record what form it takes.
- Link your observations to the Early Years Foundation Stage.
- Watch if the children engage in trial and error learning and how it develops their explorations.
- Look for evidence to show developing schemas:
  - It is a good idea to provide a large cardboard box to meet the needs of a child who may want to throw things. Throwing is a way of exploring trajectory and providing something for a toddler to throw an object into can reduce the risk of harm coming to another child or adult. Make a note of how the toddler can change from aimless 'throwing' to actually filling the box. This will involve transporting and possibly positioning.

- Connection, as the toddler joins objects together in both conventional and unconventional ways, for example not just stacking blocks onto each other, but putting hoses into tubes or plastic bottles.
- Enveloping or wrapping and transporting as objects are put carefully into different containers, moved around, wrapped in materials.
- Rotation, for example putting corks in a bottle and turning it round, rolling balls or reels over a surface or round a large container.

Children's play is complex, and during any session many different behaviours can be observed. It is through gaining an understanding of these play behaviours and closely observing children at play, that adults can really understand what is going on, and so begin to help children move on to the next stage. The terms 'ludic' and epistemic' play are used to distinguish two very different kinds of play behaviours evident in heuristic play sessions, which require different responses from adults.

Epistemic play includes acquiring knowledge and information, problem solving and exploration, finding out 'What does this object do'. This form of play is often considered as productive play as it promotes learning. Children, babies and toddlers are totally aware of and focused on what they are making, or doing and it leads to greater competence. Children need adults to support and encourage them in their discoveries; to answer questions and supply information and if asked to, become involved.

Ludic play has symbolic and fantasy elements; it is innovative and unconstrained. Actions are repeated and

Think about it

Imagine that you have been offered a food that you have never seen before. Do you pop it straight into your mouth and chew away? I doubt it. You probably will smell it, look at it closely, and if appropriate hold it, feel its texture with your tongue, all before actually eating it. In other words you use your senses to give you information and to explore and discover as much as you can.

to a certain extent it is playful and fun. Ludic play can be very dependent on the mood of the child and their levels of concentration. It does not require adults to be involved, although they should be sensitive to the child's needs. Children ask the question, 'What can I do with this object?'. Ludic play can often take place outside, in the open air as children explore their environment in a relaxed and fun way.

Heuristic play provides opportunities for both ludic and epistemic play behaviours. For example, in ludic play a child picks up a cardboard tube and it becomes a trumpet, the child makes noises, and laughs at their own invention, a child puts a chain around their neck and it becomes a necklace, in

Epistemic play

What does this object do?

Ludic play

epistemic play a child joins several boxes together with adult help and moves other objects around the room in the boxes.

What do they need?

If you have children in your setting from a very young age, they will probably have outgrown many toys and resources by the time they get to this age. In fact they can sometimes appear to be bored and disinterested by certain toys and playthings. However, this is not the case with heuristic play materials: there is always something new to discover and explore. Discovery and exploratory play is something that we never grow out of; adults and older children will still engage in this form of play, especially when presented with something new or different.

Up until now, heuristic play and treasure baskets have been solitary experiences, but now the child has other needs; they actively seek out others to play with and share their discoveries. During the third year of life children become more social and will begin to play together. This is often referred to as cooperative play. These shared experiences help to develop language and imagination as well as social skills. As language develops, they naturally want to talk about their ideas, their achievements and share them with others. In doing so the play develops at a higher level, for example a box will become more than something to transport other objects, but may become a boat, or a car; other children can participate in the play and develop it to a higher level. Both ludic and epistemic play can be observed.

Heuristic play is open-ended, there are no right or wrong ways to play as mentioned before. It therefore allows children to discover things for themselves and in doing so develop greater awareness of themselves, their capabilities and limitations. They can take risks safely and set themselves challenges, sometimes taking the initiative or, on other occasions, following the lead of others. This provides opportunities for developing positive self-esteem and self-confidence. As they share their experiences with other children they develop their ability to cooperate, share,

Case study

Lee and George, both 30 months, played with the heuristic play materials together. They copied each others actions, such as putting small objects in bottles and shaking them, lining up tins, each one going and getting one tin at a time and taking it in turns to make the line. Once they had a line of tins they then found a tube each and began to bang the tins as if they were drums.

empathise, negotiate and take turns. In this way heuristic play provides valuable opportunities for epistemic behaviours.

What do you need to collect?

The objects that you collected for heuristic play sessions for toddlers can be successfully offered to older children. They will use the materials in different ways and maybe turn them into something else, such as food, weapons, vehicles, clothes, telescopes, trumpets, tools etc. If you want to encourage more ludic play behaviours you may want to supplement the objects offered to toddlers with other materials, such as:

- Large boxes with and without lids
- Large tins with and without lids
- Large storage boxes

- Large and small sheets or pieces of material
- Large tubes
- Sheets of bubble wrap
- Silver foil
- Large pieces of paper, wallpaper, newspaper
- Things for fixing and connecting such as sellotape, parcel tape, elastic bands, string, clips
- You may also feel it appropriate to offer scissors and safety pins.

When to have a heuristic play session

Ludic play is mood dependent and so can lack focus, depending on the child. This will have a significant impact on when you organise the play session. If the child is tired, hungry, not comfortable and so on, the play will not be especially productive. As mentioned in earlier chapters you need to take into consideration all these factors when planning your sessions. Make sure that as much as possible there are no other distractions from other toys, adults or younger children.

Heuristic play can not, under any circumstances, be hurried. It is essential that you have planned sufficient time for children to explore, discover, investigate and share with others the results of their play. Clearing away is a fundamental part of the session, as with toddlers, and you should not end up doing it yourself after the children have moved on to lunch or something else. Elinor Goldschmied suggested a minimum of 45 minutes for a heuristic play session with the last 15 minutes devoted to clearing away. It is my experience, and that of other practitioners, that older children engage in heuristic play for longer periods and playing with the objects and materials for over an hour is not unusual, followed by 15 minutes clearing away time.

The role of the adult

The most important thing is to allow children to develop their own ideas. They may want to talk to you about what they are doing and you should respond appropriately by:

- Be willing to help or support the child when asked, but otherwise remain calm, still and observant.
- Recognise that it is very important that you allow the children to develop their own ideas in the first place; to talk to you about their plans and thoughts and respond appropriately. You might be asked to hold something in place whilst a child makes a connection; repair something that has fallen down or broken.
- Make sure that you provide plenty of materials and objects, and so avoid conflicts.
- As the children play, create and move objects, it is inevitable that things will become jumbled and cause confusion, maybe even limit children's explorations. When appropriate, and at a time that will not disturb the concentration of the play, subtly move materials so that they are accessible. This will promote further exploration and investigation.
- When a child asks you for support take the opportunity to 'scaffold' their play and learning, enabling them to move into the zone of proximal development. Scaffolding is when you support and extend the play through the use of open-ended questions and in doing so move the children on to the next level of their understanding. This is explained in more detail in the **Think about it** section.

Links to the Early Years Foundation Stage

Heuristic play fully supports the EYFS theme of **Enabling Environments**, as you will have created a situation within your setting that offers a range of experiences that encourage children's interest and curiosity. A heuristic play session with carefully resourced materials and objects can

Case study

Janet was watching Lee and George play, she noted that both children happily explored each collection of materials and spent time finding out what could be used to make things different, such as wrapping a wooden block with a length of ribbon. She also admitted that she didn't notice that the children were lining things up and, as she watched more carefully, became aware that this was evidence of the schema of positioning.

Think about it

The theorist, Jerome Bruner, (born 1915) argued that adults can support children's development, in particular the emotional and social aspects, by being actively involved with them whilst they play. This involvement he described as scaffolding and has been widely adopted as the reasons why we should play alongside children. However, during heuristic play, according to Elinor Goldschmied, adults should be calm, still, quiet and involved only in offering acknowledgement of achievements through smiles, nods and so on. However, children of this age are becoming more skilled both in language and creativity and so may ask you to help them. You can use these requests to 'scaffold' the child's play and learning and so extend their understanding.

Lev Vygotsky (1896-1934) was another theorist who advocated adult involvement in children's play. He suggested that all children had potential which could be unlocked by sensitive adults. He called what a child can do without adult help the 'Zone of Actual Development', (ZAD) and what the child can do with adult support 'the Zone of Proximal Development' (ZPD).

give young children real choices about what they play with and how they explore and investigate, which links to the theme **A Unique Child**.

As mentioned earlier in this section, heuristic play encourages self-confidence and self-esteem, a feature of personal, social and emotional development. Children make decisions independently and can show particular preferences and interests, for example a child may choose to spend time enveloping other objects on materials, or creating a way of transporting big objects successfully from one place to another, without adult involvement. Valuing and supporting the children in their decision making and offering encouragement when they discover new things is a fundamental part of dispositions and attitudes. The clearing away aspect of heuristic play enables young children to become aware of responsibility and self management. Through heuristic play children will begin to understand risks and challenges in their play. They will develop strategies to join in play, extend discoveries and share achievements. Because heuristic play is open-ended, and provided that you have a wealth of materials and objects, disputes are rare and so positive behaviour is encouraged and supported.

Heuristic play is often quiet and so there is the danger that we do not regard it as an opportunity to develop communication, language and literacy. However, a sensitive adult can use clearing away time to name objects and so increase vocabulary; young children playing cooperatively will share ideas, ask questions and negotiate with each other. Language skills such as turn taking and the conventions of language such as 'please' and 'thank you' can be encouraged during clearing away time. Children who have English as an additional language will be able to fully participate in heuristic play, as the play is not language dependent in the same way that role play can be. Children will begin to use language to connect their ideas, explain to others what they are doing and what they are going to do.

In the Statutory Framework for the Early Years Foundation Stage (2012) page 5 , it states: '*Understanding the world*

Case study

Oliver, aged 22 months, was engrossed in exploring large plant pots. He put them on his head, put other objects inside and transported things around the room. He discovered that he could see through the holes in the bottom of the pot and squealed with delight as he saw things differently. He shared his discovery with his carer, giving her a plant pot so that they could peer at each other through the holes. He took the plant pot away from his face and sat down. He began to explore the holes and discovered that he could get his fingers through them. His carer laughed as he wiggled his fingers and Oliver repeated these movements. He reached for a smaller pot, but couldn't get his fingers through the holes. His explorations and investigations of the properties of the plant pots continued for some time.

involves guiding children to make sense of their physical world and their community through opportunities to explore, observe and find out about people and places, technology and the environment.' There are endless opportunities for Problem solving, reasoning and numeracy during heuristic play. Children sort, match, pair up objects, become aware of similarities and difference and use mathematical language such as 'under', 'heavy', 'full', 'more'. Pairing and matching is a 'learning tool' and enables children to select and make choices, for example being able to find a beaker out of an assortment of plates, bowls and beakers. You will see children filling and emptying containers, not only is this a common schema but it is also part of their understanding of shape, space and measures.

The case study on page 36 shows how heuristic play supports the area of development and learning of knowledge and **Understanding the World**, in particular the aspect of exploration and investigation.

Children can often be observed using different objects as tools or as part of a structure, for example using a cardboard tube to support a pile of objects. They will build and construct using the larger materials such as plant pots, tins, and boxes and can often be observed amending their designs as they build and create. Piling objects on top of each other is a 'learning tool' and helps the child develop the ability to have a mental image in order to create a structure and then to actually create it.

Physical development is interlinked to all other areas of learning and heuristic play provides opportunities to challenge and extend this development. Filling big containers with objects and then trying to move them around can be challenging for a young child as the box and its contents could be quite heavy. Sensory development, fine and gross motor skills are all developed and extended through heuristic play, the greater the variety of objects and materials the greater the range of movements and skills that can be developed. The nature of heuristic play enables children to persist in their activities and practice new and existing skills.

Expressive Arts and Design is a process and does not require an end product. Heuristic play is not about making models or structures; it is open-ended and has no end product. It is truly creative at any level and is without pressure to succeed or produce. Children will respond to heuristic play in many ways. Some will express their pleasure and discoveries, like Oliver, in the case study, and squeal with delight. Others want to express themselves through words, body language or gestures. Oliver spent some time exploring the texture and material of the plant pots, he then moved over to a large tin and felt the ridged sides, he returned to the pot and felt it again, clearly exploring the different materials.

Observation and assessment suggestions and links to schemas

As with treasure baskets and heuristic play for toddlers, there are endless opportunities for observation, especially if you are not supporting or involved with the play. Children do not make one observation as they explore and investigate the materials offered; they make several as they constantly readjust their views, schemas and ideas as they observe and notice more. We should follow their example – remember one observation is never sufficient evidence to fully and accurately assess a child's understanding and, in all cases more than one observation must be carried out in order to develop a holistic view of the child.

Suggestions for observations:

- Observe a child as he or she moves objects around the room. Make a note of how they plan to move things: does it involve other children, do they ask for help? This could be used as evidence of the schema for transporting.
- When a child is engaged in heuristic play, make a note of how they use their senses: do they use all of their senses or are some more obvious than others?
- Look for evidence of fine manipulative and motor skills as children explore the materials.

- Make a note of any adult/child interactions. Who initiates it, how much interaction is there and how long it lasts. Try and link your observations to the work of Jerome Bruner and Lev Vygotsky.
- Watch the child carefully and see if they are using imagination with the materials.
- Make a note of any mathematical language that is used, especially during clearing away. Do the children use the language or do they repeat what is said by the adult?
- Look for repetition during the play session. Does the child repeat a new skill that they have just discovered; do they repeat patterns of skills that have already become established?

- Make a note of any learning tools that are evident and how are they displayed.
- Look for evidence that children have moved on in their thinking from 'What can I do with this object?' to 'What can it become?'
- Look for evidence of schemas such as:
  - **Trajectory** – which could be evident as a child waves or moves large pieces of material or paper.
  - **Positioning** – could be evident as the child attempts to pile different objects or materials on top of each other, or as they sort, pair and match.
  - **Connection** – may take on the form of joining things together with sticky tape or string; this may need adult support.
  - **Enveloping** – or wrapping, and transporting should be very evident throughout the play session.
  - **Rotation** – can be evident if you have provided materials and objects that roll, such as tubes, balls, spools.

What do they need?

Children's play is always based on their experiences, whether they are from home or from the setting. This has implications for how we resource and manage the play sessions, how we respond to the needs of the children and extend and stimulate their learning and development. Whether we agree with it or not, adults working with children of this age often feel under pressure to provide evidence of learning, such as checklists of phonics that can be repeated, or letter and number recognition. In other words: tangible outcomes. Heuristic play, and indeed treasure baskets, have no visible outcomes and for these reasons the instances of this type of play are often less frequent than with toddlers. This is a great pity as heuristic play or open-ended play, with opportunities for self-discovery, should continue throughout a child's life.

If you have offered treasure baskets and heuristic play throughout play sessions there is always the possibility that children will eventually lose interest. This could be overcome if you had access to limitless new materials to add and swap with existing materials; but most places don't. There are financial issues as well as storage and other practical considerations. Maybe you need to offer heuristic play less often, or limit the range of materials, for example by offering all metal objects, or introducing sand or water as a different medium to use with the objects. Offer heuristic play outside with large materials and objects that would not be available inside, such as large pieces of wood, big boxes and containers and long pieces of rope.

Many of the play materials offered to children are man-made with complicated machinery and do not allow the children to develop their own original and unique ways of playing with the toy. Such toys have an instant appeal, but because they do not promote creativity are often quickly discarded. Heuristic play materials do not date, or 'go out of fashion', as many commercial toys can. Another point to consider is that it will not incur vast expense on your part

Think about it

How often have you carefully gift wrapped a present for a child and when given the gift, they rip it open, give it a cursory glance and then proceed to play with the paper, gift bows and ribbon? Proof, if needed, that the most simple of materials can often stimulate quality play experiences.

and when no longer required many of the materials and objects can be recycled.

What do you need to change?

When children have reached the age when they are competent language users the treasure basket can be a great opportunity to stimulate vocabulary and language in general. Sessions can be with a small group and one adult, and can provide a fun and social activity. You can play different games with the contents of the basket, for example:

- Get the children to close their eyes and try to guess what object they can feel.
- Take out about 20 objects, possibly all made from a similar material such as metal or wood. Place on a tray and ask children to close their eyes, remove one object, and then see if the children can identify which one you have taken away.
- Again put about 15–20 objects on a tray, cover with a tray and then ask the children to recall as many as possible.
- Ask the children to choose an object from the basket and then describe what they are holding.

Other ways that you can use treasure baskets with older children are to create themed baskets. You can be really inventive and theme your basket however you like. Some baskets could be for long-term use, like the one that you would use for non-mobile babies, others can have disposable or perishable objects, such as vegetables, fruits or different types of paper. These baskets can only be used for a short period of time.

Make sure that you match the contents of the themed baskets to the age and stage of development of the children that they are intended for. Take care that if you include small objects such as coins, pebbles, small bells, toddlers and babies are not able to access the basket.

Some ideas for themed baskets:

● Different materials and textures such as:
- Fabric
- Wood
- Metal
- Rubber
- Leather
- Glass
- Paper.

Think about it

How do you feel about creating a treasure basket that has some plastic objects? Most children are surrounded by plastic everyday and it could be argued that such as basket would not have the same appeal as one filled with a more unusual collection.

● Collections of the same type of objects such as:
- Brushes
- Spoons
- Things that are the same shape such as circles, cuboids, tubes, both long and thin and small and chunky
- Things that roll
- Things that are very light
- Things that make a noise/musical sound
- Objects that are either heavy or light
- Magnetic objects
- Shells
- Objects that are hard and soft
- Vegetables
- Fruit.

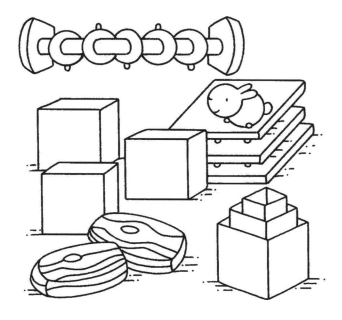

Heuristic Play

- Baskets that are associated with seasons, festivals, special events or different times of the year such as:
  - Birthdays
  - Weddings
  - New baby
  - Christmas
  - Diwali
  - Hanukkah
  - Eid
  - Spring
  - Summer
  - Winter
  - Autumn
  - Easter
  - Holidays
  - Cold weather
  - Wet weather
  - Hot weather.

- Collections linked to trips and outings such as:
  - The seaside
  - The zoo
  - Woodland or park.

- Baskets that are linked to phonic sounds.

- Collections that are linked to specific schema such as:
  - Materials and objects to encourage enveloping and wrapping
  - Materials and objects that encourage containing, e.g. putting small things in larger objects, especially with lids or tops that can be closed
  - Materials and objects that encourage connection, such as tubes that can be slotted to together, chains that can be joined together, pegs, clips etc.

- Collections that are all one specific colour.

- Collections from different rooms in the home, such as:
  - Bathroom
  - Kitchen
  - Bedroom.

Case study

The staff of a pre-school room in a day nursery had developed a range of baskets to support phonic work. These were used in small groups with perhaps just two or three children and one adult. Children were encouraged to explore the basket and name and discuss each object as they handled it. They began to associate the name of the object with the initial phonic sound. In the 'S' basket, for example, there were socks, straws, spoons, soap, string, sponge, sieves, hair slides, to mention just a few. The activity often lasted for at least 45 minutes and children displayed high levels of concentration. Staff were delighted when some of the children began to bring things in from home to add to the phonic baskets, one child brought a piece of snakeskin belonging to a grandparent, another brought a range of scented soaps. These additions promoted lots of sensory explorations and discussions about likes and dislikes.

● Collections linked to stories, rhymes and jingles.

Let your imagine run free and be creative when collecting objects for a themed treasure basket. Provided that you have checked that all the objects are safe, hygienic, clean and not damaged you can include almost anything, (provided it is not plastic). Encourage children and parents to contribute, especially if there is a cost factor involved, for example it can be quite expensive to provide 20 different types of fruit, especially as some of the more unusual ones can be pricey and this type of collection will only have a short life span. Also remember that children have different lifestyles and may, for instance, keep different things to you in their house. This will stimulate discussion and a greater awareness and respect for different lifestyles in their community.

Treasure baskets can be used very successfully with children who have additional or special educational needs. This is because treasure baskets can be enjoyed at whatever developmental level or stage a child is at. There are no prescribed outcomes and therefore no risk of failure or getting something wrong. Many children may require additional support from the adult to explore and investigate. You may have to sit alongside the child and place an object in the child's hand, but you should still be aware that you do not lead or dominate the explorations.

Children with moderate or severe physical difficulties may find that the treasure basket will stimulate manipulative and motor skills, as well as sensory development. Treasure basket play will help maintain self-esteem and self-confidence as the play is totally controlled by the child. Treasure baskets will also help in the development of schema and learning tools. Once you can identify these, you will be better equipped to meet their individual needs. You can mimic what the child is doing and then take it one stage further so that the child will copy what you have done. Treasure baskets can be placed on trays in front of wheelchairs and buggies, or on standing frames; the child can be placed on a blanket or a bean bag or whatever will meet their needs and interests.

When to have an amended heuristic play session

We have discussed the best time of day to have a heuristic or treasure basket play session in previous chapters and these features are still appropriate for older children. However, because older children often have greater use of language and are more independent, they may choose themed treasure basket play at almost anytime of day. If you are aware that there is only limited time for the activity, you must point this out to the children, but not reject their decisions. This age of child will frequently be content to have a short session and then return to the activity at a different time, especially if this is explained to them appropriately.

Don't restrict the exploration of themed baskets to indoors. Children can investigate and explore anywhere. This type of activity can be very successfully undertaken sitting in the shade on a warm day. In the same way, if your basket has a collection of heavy and light objects children may want to extend their discoveries to include a water tray and investigate floating and sinking. A collection of objects that make a noise, musical or otherwise, can often be very successful outside and children may be able to create different sounds by banging things on the ground, grass, or walls in a safe environment.

The role of the adult

Children of this age often have well developed epistemic play behaviours and can concentrate for long periods of time. There is little need for adult intervention during their play and in many cases this could disturb the child's concentration, or the opportunity to learn something new independently. However, adults are needed for support, encouragement and help if asked for.

- Make sure that you replace perishable objects, such as fruit and vegetables, or disposable objects, such as paper, card and foil, as soon as they appear worn or bruised. If you don't do this the basket will lose its appeal and interest.
- Be prepared for older children to taste or bite some of the fruit and vegetables; remember that this is first and foremost a sensory activity. You might not want to bite into a raw onion for example, but is that good enough reason to stop a child? The question of the fruit or vegetable being 'dirty' should never arise if you have prepared your basket properly.
- Make sure that you wash or wipe all items after each play session. As with clearing away time for heuristic play, there is no reason why older children can't be involved in the cleaning of objects in the basket.
- Be prepared to offer support, perhaps by naming different objects or encouraging children to explore in different ways, such as holding different materials up to the light and looking through them.

- Try as much as is possible to allow plenty of time for children to explore the baskets. Baskets that are designed to promote schema for example, can engage a child for a considerable length of time. It can be very frustrating to have discoveries interrupted because of lack of time.
- Allow children, as much as your setting permits, to have free access to the baskets and allow them to have freedom of choice in the way they select the objects to investigate.
- Children need to have freedom to plan how they will explore the objects in the basket, so it is important that you are flexible and prepared to accept changes.
- If playing 'games' with a treasure basket make sure that the objects stay inside the basket and are not taken out, other than for the purpose of exploration and investigation. Don't let the objects become props for other forms of play such as pretend, role or imaginative.

Links to the Early Years Foundation Stage

Treasure baskets can be linked to all areas of the EYFS and therefore can become a fundamental part of your planning and assessment of the children's development and learning.

Treasure baskets will help a child to continue to be motivated, interested and excited by their learning. They will help the child gain confidence to try new activities and develop good concentration skills. These are important aspects of personal, social and emotional development; in addition, if the baskets are offered to a small group, children will gain a greater awareness of each other, take turns and develop patience. As adults have a limited role during the actual session, treasure baskets encourage the child to select and use the materials and objects independently. In communication, language and literacy, themed baskets will help to develop and extend a child's vocabulary. As they explore objects they will also get opportunities to explore sounds and meanings; they could link letters and sounds (especially with phonic themed baskets) and sound out letters of the alphabet. Depending on

the theme of the basket there maybe opportunities to use language to imagine and recreate roles and personal experiences as well as those of others. Story baskets encourage children to retell stories in their own words and recall events.

Mathematics – older children can often count confidently up to five, and many to ten. Opportunities to use number names in familiar contexts, such as counting the number of brushes or shells, are endless with treasure baskets. Similarly, using mathematical language will come very naturally with themed baskets, such as heavy and light, bigger and smaller, more and less; as well as using language to describe the position of objects such as next to, under, above, beside. With support and encouragement children may begin to combine two groups of objects; this is the basis of addition, subtraction and calculation. Again, depending on the theme of the baskets there may be opportunities to become aware of patterns, for example how bristles are put into the head of a brush and how they differ in other brushes.

'Development Matters' (2012) tells us that to provide an enabling environment practitioners should '*provide a wide range of materials, resources and sensory experiences to enable children to explore colour, texture and space.*' (page 43). This summarises the philosophy of themed treasure basket sessions with older children completely.

As children explore and investigate they are using all of their senses; they will develop coordination, balance and learn how to handle a range of objects and materials with control and in a safe manner. All of these are important aspects of **Physical Development**. Themed baskets, such as bathroom, kitchen etc., can help children develop an understanding of keeping healthy and an awareness of good hygiene practices.

Expressive Arts and Design is about having a go, taking risks, learning new things and being adventurous. Some of the themed baskets that you collect may contain objects that the children have never seen or encountered before, such as some fruits and vegetables, these experiences will extend and stimulate their learning and development. Baskets could help children explore colour, shape and textures in both two and three dimensions. The children will respond in their own unique ways to their explorations: sometimes using all of their sense, sometimes remain quiet: sometimes displaying emotions such as excitement, wariness, joy, frustration.

Observation and assessment suggestions and links to schemas

Many of the observation suggestions from earlier sections can be adapted for this age group, but remember you are not comparing children, and each observation should focus on the unique qualities and skills of an individual child.

● Observe the levels of concentration and attentiveness during the play session and also at another activity. Compare the length of time taken exploring the basket with the second activity.

- Make a note of how the child works as part of a small group: do they take turns, share – not just the objects, but the attention of the adult.
- Can you see evidence in your observations that a child has an awareness of a sense of community? When exploring a themed basket it may contain objects that they are not familiar with in their own home; do they show interest and respect for different ways of life? This can also be linked to **Understanding the World**; how do they express their views of different lifestyles?
- Make a note of the language a child uses to tell you or others about their investigations, or to recall a special event such as a wedding, or a birthday.
- Observe a child counting, problem solving and using mathematical language. Make a note of how they decide which objects are heavy or light, whether there are more or less items.
- Observe a child exploring and investigating a new or different object. What questions do they ask, how do they explore, do they use all of their senses, and how do they respond to challenge?
- Look for evidence of schemas, for example:
  - Does the child take things out of the basket and line them up on some order – positioning?
  - Does the child make attempts to make connections; such as tying together all cutlery, from a kitchen-themed basket?
  - Can you see evidence of rotation as a child turns keys, knobs, wheels?
  - Enveloping and containing may be observed as a child puts small objects inside larger ones.
- If you give a treasure basket to a child with additional or special educational needs, you can think about the following observations:
  - Does the child show pleasure, and if so how is this manifested?
  - Does the child show anxiety or fear about the objects and again how is this manifested?
  - Does the child 'mouth' the objects to explore their features?
  - Does the child use all of their senses (where appropriate) to explore and investigate?

- Does the child initiate any interactions with the adult, or do they seek adult reassurance?
- Is there any repetition in the play and what does this indicate to you?
- How long does the session last: is it longer or shorter than normal?

Observation templates

How to use the observation and planning Proforma 1

This is intended to be a summary sheet which will enable you to assess a child's progress and plan the next steps over about a month or so. In the first instance you undertake a series of focused observations, maybe five or six, in any appropriate format on one child. Then write a summary of your findings in the box on the top left and use the column on the right to link the information to the areas of learning and development. It does not matter if you do not have evidence to link to all six areas; in fact it would be very surprising if you did.

Look carefully at your findings and identify two or three skills that are clearly evident. Remember to focus on achievement, what the child **can do**, rather than on what they can't do. The EYFS guidance suggests that we should make systematic observations that take into consideration each child's interests, achievements and learning styles. Don't try to identify too many skills, otherwise it will become overwhelming for both you and the child, and realistically you would not be able to successfully plan experiences and activities to cover a multitude of skills. By focusing on a small number it will be manageable and achievable.

Our learning style is the way we process information and make sense of experiences in which we are involved.

There are four main learning styles:

- **Visual** – a preference for using pictures, demonstrations and watching others speak as well as listen.
- **Auditory** – a preference for using sounds and music, and for hearing the spoken word and different voices.
- **Tactile** – a preference for touching, handling and experimentation, as well as for using drawings or diagrams to supplement learning.
- **Kinaesthetic** – preference for using the body and hands to touch and examine.

The way we learn – our learning style – will vary for each individual and children may combine different learning styles in different situations or at different stages of their development. We all have a mix of learning styles, but often there will be one that is dominant. The box on the bottom right of the summary sheet suggests that you try to identify a learning style; if you can do this you will be able to plan more meaningful experiences for the child.

The arrow leads you to the box on the bottom left where you can briefly outline activities and experiences that will enable the child to progress. You also identify your role, which can be linked to resources needed, observation opportunities, time management or anything else you deem to be relevant. The next step for you is to provide the activities and experiences, do a series of observations, and then the whole process begins again on a second sheet.

Name _____ Date of birth _____

Date of observation _____ Completed by _____

Observation notes, photos, sticky notes

Links to

Communication
and Language

Physical Development

Personal, Social
and Emotional
Development

Literacy

Mathematics

Understanding
the World

Expressive Arts
and Design

Planning – What experiences or opportunities can be provided to support the learning and/or skill development?

Reflection – Which skills can be observed

What is the role of the adult?

Can you identify a learning style?

Positive relationships
Enabling environments

Learning and development

**Practical
Pre-School Books**
www.practicalpreschoolbooks.com

Observation templates

How to use the observation and planning proforma 2

Again, this is a proforma that can be used over a period of time and is designed to support sustained shared thinking. It is intended that this sheet would be used with a child who can verbally express their interests. Together, you and the child identify an interest which is written in the inner circle; both of you think of activities and experiences that would satisfy this interest, usually about five or six. For example, a child may say that they like building things (this would be written in the inner circle), activities to be written in the middle circle could be a heuristic play session, stories and rhymes about building and constructing things, visiting a building site, exploring large building materials such a bricks, breezeblocks, pipes, role play. All of these activities would involve other children, so although they stem from one particular child's interest there will still be opportunities to develop relationships with other children and adults. Another child may have a particular interest in books so there would-be an overlap of provision, and in the same way another may enjoy role play. Not all of these activities have to be provided at every session, but it is suggested that one, such as heuristic play, would be available all the time. This is referred to as 'continuous provision'.

In the outer circle you can make brief observation notes during the course of each activity and make links to the seven areas of learning and development. In this way your observation will be focused. For example, if you observe the child during a story or rhyme time, you could directly link your observation to communication and language; observing the child exploring large building materials could be linked to understanding the world or expressive arts and design.

Outside of the circle you can record decisions about how you could extend the learning and development and then on the reverse of the sheet make a note of your plans.

Remember a child's interests can change as they develop and grow and so you will need to work together to develop a new sheet.

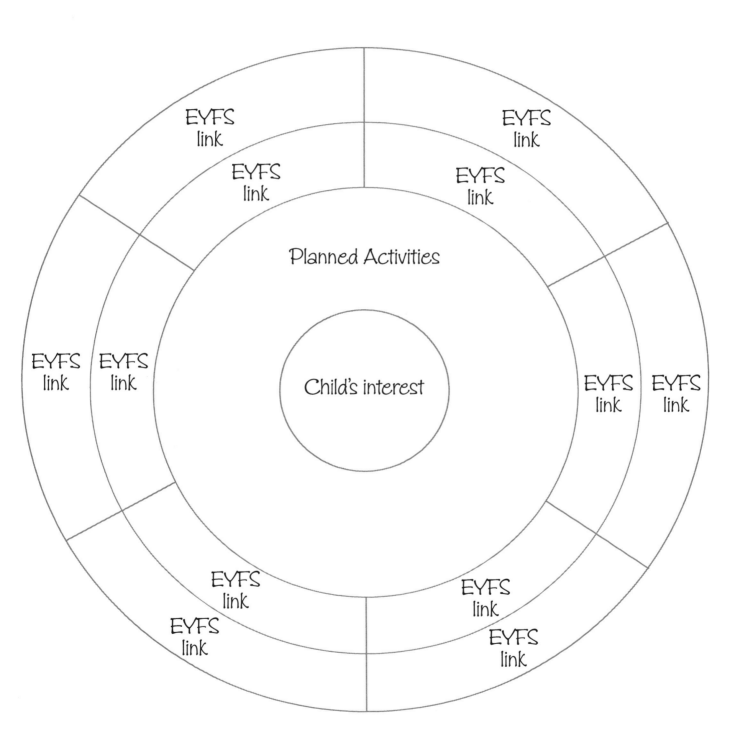

Inner circle – Child's particular interests or needs

Middle circle – Planned activities to meet interests or needs

Outer circle – Observed evidence that links to the EYFS

Heuristic Play

Glossary of terms

Assessment – a measurement or judgement about a child's learning development and acquisition of skills.

Cognitive development – intellectual growth, how children learn.

Didactic – resources that are considered to be educational, usually in a teaching situation etc.

Epistemic play – acquiring knowledge and information, problem-solving and exploration.

EYFS – Early Years Foundation Stage.

Heuristic – to discover, explore and investigate.

Holistic – considering a whole person or issue.

Learning style – the way an individual processes information.

Learning tools – the earliest patterns of behaviour that emerge in very young babies.

Ludic play – play that has symbolic or fantasy elements, as well as repetition.

Observation – watching, listening and noting the activities and responses of a child in a given situation (Look, listen and note).

Planning cycle – a circular approach to planning, observation and assessment. This usually starts with observation leads to assessment which leads planning appropriate activities.

Scaffolding – when you support and extend the play through the use of open-ended questions and your

own actions, and in doing so move the children on the next level of their understanding.

Schema – an early concept or idea based on linked patterns of behaviour.

Symbolic play – when a child can use one object to represent another and understand that the object has not changed, for example putting a banana to the ear and pretending its a telephone.

Theorist – usually an academic, living or dead, who has extensively researched a new idea and produced an original and unique point of view.

Treasure basket – a collection of natural objects offered to non-mobile babies.

Zone of Actual Development (ZAD) – the point at which most children play, learn and develop without adults or other children extending their experiences (ie. without scaffolding).

Zone of Proximal Development (ZPD) – the point children attain in their play with the support of adults or other children.

Books

Daly, M. et al.(2006) *Understanding Early Years Theory in Practice*, Heinemann.

Hughes, A. (2006) *Developing Play for the Under 3s: The treasure basket and heuristic play*, David Fulton.

Roberts, A. and Featherstone, S. (2002) *The Little Book of Treasure Baskets*, Featherstone Education.

Ridall-Leech, S. (2008) *How to Observe Children (2nd edition)*, Heinemann.

Guidance

Department for Education and Skills (2007) *Early Years Foundation Stage: Setting the standards for learning, development and care for children from birth to five* (www.foundationyears.org.uk/early-years-foundation-stage-2012).

Department for Education (2012) *Statutory Framework for the Early Years Foundation Stage: Setting the standards for learning, development and care for children from birth to five* (www.foundationyears.org.uk/early-years-foundation-stage-2012).

DfCSF (2009) *The National Strategy, Early Years – Learning, Playing and Interacting, Good Practice in the Early Years* (http://webarchive.nationalarchives.gov.uk/20110809091832/ http://www.teachingandlearningresources.org.uk)

Development Matters in the Early Years Foundation Stage (2012) (The British Association for Early Childhood Education) (http://www.foundationyears.org.uk/early-years-foundation-stage-2012/).

DVDs

Goldschmied, E. (1992) *Heuristic Play with Objects*, NCB (http://resources.ncb.org.uk/resources/publications/view-publication?PubID=571).

Goldschmied, E. (1989) *Infants at work*, NCB (http://resources.ncb.org.uk/resources/publications/view-publication?PubID=572).

Websites

www.foundationyears.org.uk

http://www.education.gov.uk/

Acknowledgements

Very special thanks to Lucy Cripps, Oliver Williams, Poppy Ellison and Phoebe Lawson, and their parents, for agreeing to be photographed and providing invaluable material for this book.

Thanks also to Janet Austin for allowing me to set up a heuristic play session in her setting.

Unless mentioned above all other names have been changed to maintain confidentiality.

Notes